PACHYCEPHALOSAURUS

by Janet Riehecky
illustrated by Llyn Hunter

THE CHILD'S WORLD

MANKATO, MN

*Grateful appreciation is expressed to
Bret S. Beall, Research Consultant,
Field Museum of Natural History, Chicago,
Illinois, who reviewed this book to
insure its accuracy.*

Library of Congress Cataloging in Publication Data

Riehecky, Janet, 1953-
    Pachycephalosaurus / by Janet Riehecky ; illustrated by Llyn
Hunter.
        p. cm. — (Dinosaur books)
    Summary: Describes known and hypothesized information about the
dinosaur Pachycephalosaurus, including its discovery, physical
appearance, and lifestyle.
    ISBN 0-89565-632-9
    1. Pachycephalosaurus—Juvenile literature.
[1. Pachycephalosaurus.   2. Dinosaurs.]   I. Hunter, Llyn, ill.
II. Title.   III. Series: Riehecky, Janet, 1953-   Dinosaur books.
QE862.065R535   1990
567.9'7—dc20   90-42519
                                                                CIP
                                                                AC

1 2 3 4 5 6 7 8 9 10 11 12 R 98 97 96 95 94 93 92 91

PACHYCEPHALOSAURUS

What were dinosaurs *really* like? No one can say for sure. There were no people around back then to see what dinosaurs looked like or how they lived.

But that doesn't stop scientists from wanting to figure out what dinosaurs were like. They study the fossils dinosaurs left behind, and they watch how animals of today behave. Their studies give them many ideas.

When scientists studied the legs of some dinosaurs, they found that those legs were long and strong. They pictured those dinosaurs running swiftly and gracefully, like ostriches.

When scientists saw the spikes and horns some plant eaters had, they imagined those dinosaurs fighting fiercely if they were attacked.

Scientists found footprints from large dinosaurs showing just their toeprints. They pictured those dinosaurs swimming in a lake, pushing themselves along with the tips of their toes, just as hippopotamuses do.

And when scientists studied the sharp
teeth, strong jaws, and vicious claws of
other dinosaurs, they knew those dinosaurs were fierce hunters.

But when scientists found the strange skull of the Pachycephalosaurus (PAK-EE-SEF-a-loh-sawr-us), they didn't know what to think at first. The top of this unusual dinosaur's head was ten inches of solid bone! That means that the bone on the top of its skull was thicker than your whole head. Why would a dinosaur need such a thick head? Well, most scientists now think that it was a built-in crash helmet. They think the Pachycephalo-saurus liked to go around crashing its head into things!

Why would a dinosaur go around crashing into things? Did it bang its head into a cliff in the morning in order to wake up? Probably not. No animal we know of does such a thing. But there are animals that bang their heads into each other.

Animals such as sheep and goats have head-butting contests within their herds. Why? To decide which animal in the herd is the strongest. A herd needs a strong leader to defend it against danger. The winner of the contest gets to be the leader. Scientists think Pachycephalosaurs had similar contests.

Scientists have also suggested several other uses that Pachycephalosaurs might have had for their crash-helmet heads. Some animals today fight to decide which one gets to live in a certain area. Two Pachycephalosaurs may have banged heads to see which one would win a territory they both wanted.

And if two bachelor Pachycephalosaurs wanted the fairest female in the flock, they might have had a head-crashing contest to see who got the girl.

It is also possible that Pachycephalo-saurs charged headfirst at enemies. They needed some defense against meat eaters, and they didn't have any horns or claws.

But there is a problem with that idea. Most meat eaters had very sharp claws. If a Pachycephalosaurus got close enough to ram a meat eater with its head, the meat eater could have slashed at its soft throat or belly. If the Pachycephalosaurus had the time to make a choice, it was better off to RUN!

Scientists have not found a complete skeleton of the Pachycephalosaurus, so they can't say for sure what this strange dinosaur looked like, except for its head. Scientists have, however, found skeletons of smaller dinosaurs with very similar heads. They believe the Pachycephalosaurus looked much like these smaller dinosaurs.

Scientists believe the Pachycephalo-saurus walked on two strong back legs. They think it had short front legs which it used as arms for grabbing plants to eat. Based on the enormous sizes of the skulls that were found, scientists believe this dinosaur grew to a length of twenty-six feet and stood more than twice as tall as a person.

Scientists think the Pachycephalo-saurus had a long, thick tail that helped to balance its body as it ran. They also think that its backbone was especially strong. Some scientists believe the dinosaur could hold its back quite stiffly, like a battering ram. This would have kept it from hurting itself when it crashed its head into some-thing.

strong, thick tail

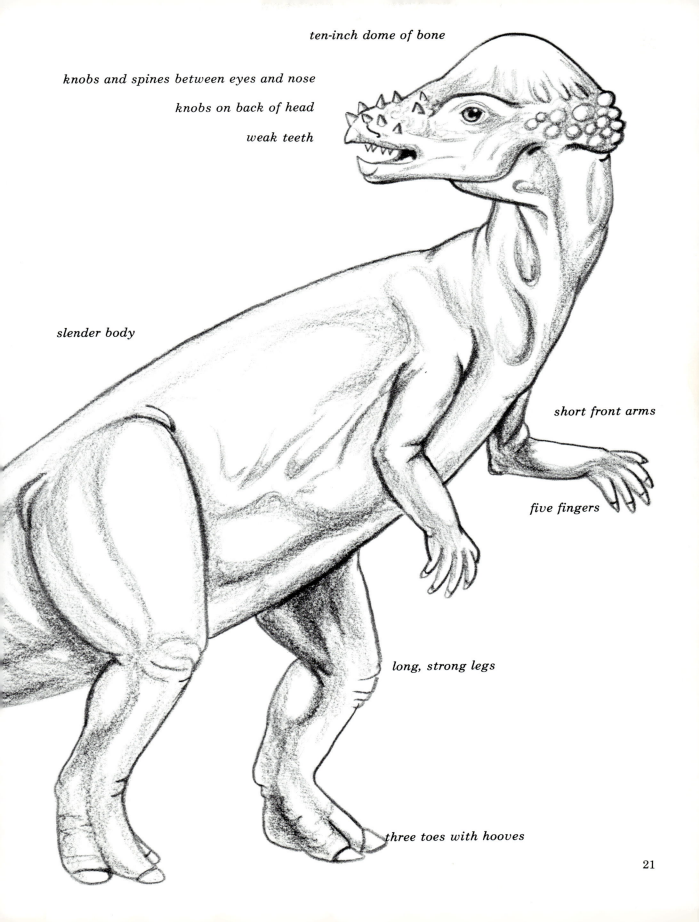

ten-inch dome of bone

knobs and spines between eyes and nose

knobs on back of head

weak teeth

slender body

short front arms

five fingers

long, strong legs

three toes with hooves

21

When scientists draw pictures of what they think the Pachycephalosaurus looked like, they imagine it as an average-looking dinosaur—except for its head.

The name Pachycephalosaurus means "thick-headed lizard." But its "crash helmet" was not the only unusual thing about this dinosaur's head.

On the back of the Pachycephalosaurus' head were many knobs of bone. They formed a pattern of large bumps, like huge warts, across the back of its head. In the front, between the eyes and the nose, were knobs and spines. These made the Pachycephalosaurus a nasty-looking dinosaur. Looking ugly may have helped the Pachycephalosaurus scare enemies away—and maybe female Pachycephalosaurs liked bumps and spines!

The nickname for Pachycephalosaurs, and dinosaurs with similar heads, is "bone-heads." That's a good nickname for them. Not only did they all have thick bone on top of their heads, but they also had very small brains. Their thick skulls didn't leave much room for brains.

Because the Pachycephalosaurus had such a small brain, scientists think it was not very smart. But then, if it had been smart, surely it wouldn't have gone around crashing its head all the time!

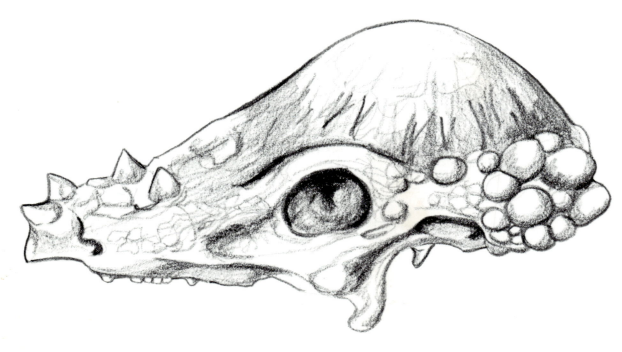

Although we can't say for sure how smart the Pachycephalosaurus was, we can be pretty sure it was at least smart enough to try to stay away from meat eaters. Some scientists think it avoided meeting up with meat eaters by living in

the hills or mountains. A Tyrannosaurus wasn't likely to go to all the work of hiking up steep hills when it was easy enough to find tasty duckbilled dinosaurs close at hand.

Scientists think that Pachycephalo-saurs roamed the hills in herds, like many other plant-eating dinosaurs. This, too, would have given them some protection. And it gave them somebody to bang heads with!

Scientists are only guessing when they describe the kind of life they think the Pachycephalosaurus and other dinosaurs lived. No one ever watched real dinosaurs. But scientists don't just make up any-

thing they want to. They base their ideas
on clues from fossils and what they know
about how animals that are alive today
behave. They may make some mistakes,
but they keep trying to find answers.

Their careful study helps us to imagine what the dinosaurs were really like!

Dinosaur Fun

The color an animal is can be a big help. It can hide an animal that doesn't want to be seen. Or it can make an animal look special to another animal in search of a mate. You can learn a lot about animals and color by reading books, such as *Animal Camouflage* by Janet McDonnell.

Since no one knows what colors dinosaurs were, draw pictures of your favorite dinosaurs and color them the way you think they might have been. Can you explain why you chose the colors you did and how those colors might have helped the dinosaurs?